A BEMERTON ANTHOLGY

poems of George Herbert
selected by Barbara Murray

and
poems of Barbara Murray

edited and with drawings by Guy Ottewell

Poems of Barbara Murray © 2010 by Barbara Murray, 2016 by Guy Ottewell
Printed in the United States of America
First published February 2010
Reprinted August 2014
2nd edition June 2016, with one added poem

ISBN 978-0-934546-57-7

The picture on the cover is of Salisbury cathedral seen across the river, from a point on the way out to Bemerton.

Universal Workshop
www.UniversalWorkshop.com

contents

4	preface
11	poems of George Herbert
27	poems of Barbara Murray

Preface

Barbara Murray once asked me to help her with a project:

> I would like to put out a choice of George Herbert's poems which are all great favorites of mine, along with a short well-written introduction. George Herbert spent his last few years in a small cottage at Bemerton, a few miles from Salisbury and easily reached through fields which lead past an eight hundred year old mill (now a pub) and give beautiful vistas of the cathedral. It was from here that Constable painted his famous views of the cathedral, which has the tallest spire in England. Nearby is the great house where lived Herbert's kinsman, the Earl of Pembroke, William Herbert, a possible contender for Shakespeare's Mr. W.H. . . . It would be lovely to have a drawing of George Herbert's house, right on the main street (actually I think there's only one street). It is directly opposite the little stone church where George was priest, and both are right against the street. On the house there is this verse he had carved:
>
>> If you chance to find
>> A good house to your mind
>> And built without your cost,
>> Be good to the poor
>> As God gives you store,
>> And then my labour's not lost.

Someone lives in the house of course, but it can be easily painted or sketched from the street. The church is of course accessible all the way round and inside and out. Last time I was there I had a lovely talk to a parishioner. I think it would be an interesting expedition for you, and it would be neat to have a frontispiece in color.... They wouldn't need to be all sketches of Bemerton. For instance, there is one [poem] called The Flower, and it needs a drawing of a daffodil (or other bulb) coming up out of the ground and another showing full bloom.... (I feel pretty sure that's what he was thinking about—there are seven pages of daffodils in Gerard's Herbal of 1633.)

Barbara said that this now interested her more than the phonic readers for children which I had insisted on printing for her.

I went to Salisbury, cycled to Bemerton and made drawings. Bemerton is halfway between Salisbury and Wilton, westward along the valley of the Nadder, one of the four rivers that meet at Salisbury. At Wilton (which gave its name to the county of Wiltshire) is Wilton House, the enormous place that was the seat of George Herbert's cousin the Earl of Pembroke and is now open to the public. From Salisbury out to Bemerton lie parallel the busy modern highway, the railway, the older road, and water meadows threaded by footpaths that interlace with the Nadder and its several side-channels. Bemerton village lines the older road. The tiny church is on the north side; dominating it from across the road is the house built by Herbert. There had been a smaller rectory on the site since 1470; as restored by Herbert it is not a "small cottage" but a rambling mansion, with extensive garden straddling the river. The current owner gave me a glossy sale booklet. I spent a day going to and fro and making drawings, though they were perhaps not quite what Barbara visualized for decorations to the pages.

Her conception was of a small volume that would be in place at church and cathedral bookstores (she had several in mind). Her introductory essay, which would have justified this publication, cannot now be found, her attention departed from the project, but I want to bring it to reality for her as best I can.

She said she had chosen forty of Herbert's poems and would type them and send them, but got only as far as sending ten ("Note: Order as in my 1703 book"), and later the first two and last two stanzas of "The Flower."

They make a slim book. I want to add to it the group of her own poems—very different from George Herbert's—that she sent me,

5

neatly typed on separate sheets, "in order of composition." This, I realize, departs from her original conception, but I think it adds another kind of value.

Barbara had a mind that remembered every poem she saw. In her childhood in New Zealand, when children were made to learn poems and recite them in class—a task that other children dread and stumble over—she memorized any poem at a glance and recited it effortlessly (making herself, no doubt, acidly envied). Her childhood friend was Fleur Adcock, and she knew other New Zealand poets, Alistair Campbell and James K. Baxter. Later, besides countless poems—and countless trivia, such as scraps of advertising or popular ditties or her own parodies of them—she knew countless songs and sang many of them to her own accompaniment on her piano or on the harpsichord that was built for her: English and Scottish and New Zealand ballads, madrigals, Purcell (she had once sung the part of Dido in Victoria University of Wellington's production of *Dido and Aeneas*). Half of her library is her poetry collection. If books were being given away she would accept "any volumes of poetry." (Yet she donated to Furman University not only her harpsichord but her 1703 edition of Herbert, her "most treasured possession.") Her favorite, I had thought, was Gerard Manley Hopkins. She also understood poetry, as fast and easily as she read.

Some people, I think, create stuff uncritically, generate words or sketches or other artifacts without much inhibition, and criticize and improve their product later, if at all. I'm of that kind. Others are of the opposite tendency. It could be called realism. They see all too well what they are doing, as and if they try to do it, and this can be a discouragement to doing it at all. Barbara allowed herself to produce things few, small, and faultless: teaching materials for Montessori schoolchildren, drawings of flowers, and poems.

Most of the poems are, as true poetry is, driven by real feeling and crafted out of surprisingly found words. The first few, which happen to be bitter personal reproaches, seem to me the most necessitated, meant, in any language. Beside them, many other poems seem to be acts of play that could have been left undone.

"Despite Us" was my name for a series of drawings of roots pushing sidewalks up, grass growing in drains, ant cities emerging through asphalt, and the like. Barbara misheard it, and preferred it, as "Despiters." Her "too unthrifty" is perhaps an intended ambiguity, or a combination of both its meanings into the word "too."

"They laid her in the garden": Barbara created this memorial garden for St. James Church on Piney Mountain in Greenville.

The poem by Philippe Desportes was sent to me just for possible use as a filler in my *Astronomical Calendar*. It and her translation are in faded longhand on pages of school paper, now browned and fragile. I decided to add them here because the translation is superb. It maintains the rhyme-scheme of the sonnet (by, for instance, switching the places of the words *tomb* and *sepulchre*); and since French classical verse has twelve syllables to the line and English ten, it has to say the same in less material—yet ends with a dodecasyllable as if to signal its French source. The word "soaring" just might be, as I at first read it, "searing," which would also be appropriate for the encounter of Icarus with the sun. The eleventh line seemed to have been mis-copied: shouldn't the last three words be plural? The solution turned out to be that the only slip was *les* instead of *des*. The French disentangles as: "He had, to burn him, the loveliest of stars," meaning the sun. The sun looms over the story, yet is only thus indirectly mentioned—*soleil* is never used. (And *des astres* reminds us, whether intentionally or not, of the identically pronounced *désastre*, "disaster.") It may be that the young translator also failed to disentangle this idea, and therefore brought in a different one. This line has to rhyme with the last. Rhyming with identically sounding syllables (*beau . . . tombeau*) is avoided in English, but in French is called *rime riche* and regarded as a capping achievement. —Icarus and his father Daedalus symbolize many things. I have just been told of a poem by Jack Gilbert called "Failing and Flying" on the theme of (Tennyson's) "better to have loved and lost than never to have loved at all": "Everyone forgets that Icarus also flew . . . I believe Icarus was not failing as he fell, / but just coming to the end of his triumph."

On the reverse of Barbara's two pages are other pieces more obviously juvenile, though with touches of originality such as "Cutting the day, dividing it in pieces." I did not think of including these, till persuaded by her children ("The poems may be simple, but they are still better than most of the dreck published in [a famous magazine] . . ."). "Canterbury Plains" is annotated "(Begun April, finished June)" and must have continued on another page; the other two poems are crossed out, and "You Who Are Gay" is annotated "(Incomplete version with middle verse see 3 leaves on)."

Philippe Desportes was an older contemporary (1546–1606) of George Herbert, but a lighter poet. He was a courtier of Henry III; who was an interesting person, briefly king of what was then the combined Commonwealth of Poland and Lithuania (a state larger than Russia), then king of France, and murdered by a religious fanatic four years before George Herbert's birth.

George Herbert (1593–1633) was born into a rich family that had many branches throughout southern Wales; cousins of his were Earls of Pembroke and Powis, and he was born at the family's castle of Montgomery.

When he was three his father, Sir Richard, Lord of Cherbury, died and his mother, Lady Magdalen, was left to bring up ten children. She was a cultured woman, and twenty-year friend of John Donne, most dazzling exponent of the school of poetry that later came to be called metaphysical. She married a second husband, Sir John Danvers, twenty years her junior. George was devoted to her, and his earliest known poems were two sonnets he sent her when he was sixteen, on the theme that poetry should concern not the love of woman but the love of God. By then he was a scholar at Cambridge. He rose to become "public orator" of the university, and member of Parliament for Montgomeryshire. This could have been the springboard to a political career; but after some hesitation he entered the church, and was parish priest at Bemerton from 1630 to his death only two and a half years later. Very unlike idle and greedy priests of the time, he gave food and clothes to the poor among his parishioners, took the sacraments to them when they were ill. He had married Ann Danvers, a cousin of his stepfather. George and Ann had no children of their own, but took into their home the three orphaned daughters of one of his sisters. At Bemerton he wrote his prose work *The Priest to the Temple*, on the duties of a parish priest; and collections of proverbs, of which we remember "His bark is worse than his bite"; translated some devotional works from other languages; and composed the majority of his surviving poems, including some in Greek and Latin. (Barbara: "My explanation of this industry is that he well knew he did not have long to live.") His subjects were entirely religious. At least one has become a familiar hymn: "Let all the world in every corner sing, / My God and King." He is classified as one of the metaphysical poets. And his poems tend to be as rich as Donne's in intricate logic and metaphor (though without Donne's rampant eros). He drew up a collection of them in a manuscript volume with title *The Temple*, suggesting a resemblance between their metrical patterns and church architecture. Dying of tuberculosis, he sent this volume to Nicholas Ferrar, founder of a religious community at Little Gidding (familiar to us now as the title of one of T.S. Eliot's *Four Quartets*) in what was then Huntingdonshire and is now part of Cambridgeshire. Herbert asked Ferrar to burn the volume unless he felt it might "turn to the advantage of any dejected poor soul." Ferrar published it that year, with a preface describing its author's saintly character.

In his time George Herbert was somewhat known as a poet to a limited circle, but one among his four brothers was more prominent, besides having a longer and more colorful life: the eldest, Edward Lord Herbert of Cherbury, who was born nine years earlier and died fifteen years later. Edward traveled in Europe as a soldier and then ambassador for King James I, was clever, got into fights, and wrote a candid *Autobiography* of this adventurous period. It ended in 1624, after which this Herbert, too, lived studiously and contemplatively, though more grandly, at Montgomery Castle. When the Civil War broke out between king and Parliament, Edward loved neither side, tried to remain neutral, but in 1644 admitted Parliamentarian troops to the castle and was denounced by the Royalists as "treacherous Herbert." He wrote some histories (a life of Henry VIII), a book of poems published thirty-two years after his brother's, and *De Veritate* ("On Truth"), which for him was the important work of his life. Truth was to be sought not through revelation but through reason (of which he attempted to detail the methods). The truth he arrived at was religious (he is regarded as the founder in England of the shade of thought called Deism). But Herbert of Cherbury, brother of the gentle poet, was a stepping-stone from the seventeenth-century world of religious war and persecution toward a hoped-for world of reason and toleration.

Guy Ottewell

Note to 2016 edition: The poem "Nature Note," typed on a thinner kind of paper, somehow escaped my attention before and is now added (page 38).

George Herbert

Bemerton from the west: the small church, and opposite to it George Herbert's great rectory. (This was my first sketch; a cricket game was in progress on the field behind me.)

The village street seen from the east; a few hours later so the shadows have changed. House and church are not really so close, though they seem that way.

REDEMPTION

Having been tenant long to a rich Lord,
Not thriving, I resolvèd to be bold,
And make a suit unto him, to afford
A new small-rented Lease and cancel th'old.
In Heaven, at his Manor I him sought:
They told me there, that he was lately gone
About some land, which he had dearly bought
Long since on Earth, to take possession.
I straight return'd, and knowing his great Birth,
Sought him accordingly in great resorts;
In Cities, Theatres, Gardens, Parks and Courts:
At length I heard a ragged noise and mirth
Of Thieves and Murderers: there I him espied,
Who straight, *Your suit is granted*, said, and died.

from EASTER

I got me Flowers to strew thy way;
I got me Boughs off many a Tree:
But thou wast up by break of day,
And brought'st thy sweets along with thee.

The Sun arising in the East,
Though he give light, and th'East perfume;
If they should offer to contest
With thy arising, they presume.

Can there be any day but this,
Though many Suns to shine endeavour?
We count three hundred, but we miss:
There is but one, and that one ever.

Weathercock on the roof of George Herbert's house.

PRAYER

Prayer the Churches banquet, Angels age,
Gods breath in man returning to his birth,
The soul in paraphrase, heart in pilgrimage,
The Christian plummet sounding Heav'n and Earth;

Engine against th'Almighty, sinners tow'r,
Reversed thunder, Christ side-piercing spear,
The six-days world-transposing in an hour,
A kind of tune, which all things hear and fear;

Softness, and peace, and joy, and love, and bliss,
Exalted Manna, gladness of the best,
Heaven in ordinary, Man well drest,
The milky way, the bird of Paradise,

Church-bells beyond the stars heard, the souls blood,
The land of spices, something understood.

HOLY COMMUNION

Not in rich furniture, or fine array,
Nor in a wedge of gold,
Thou, who from me wast sold,
To me dost now thy self convey;
For so thou should'st without me still have been,
Leaving within me sin:

But by the way of nourishment and strength,
Thou creep'st into my breast;
Making thy way my rest,
And thy small quantities my length;
Which spread their Forces into every part,
Meeting sins force and art.

ANTIPHON

Let all the world in every corner sing,
    My God and King.

The heavens are not too high,
His Praise may thither fly:
The Earth is not too low,
His Praises there may grow.

Let all the world in every corner sing,
    My God and King.

The Church with Psalms must shout,
No door can keep them out:
But above all, the Heart
Must bear the longest part.

Let all the world in every corner sing,
    My God and King.

THE WINDOWS

Lord, how can man preach thy eternal word?
He is a brittle crazy glass:
Yet in thy temple thou dost him afford
This glorious and transcendent place,
To be a window, through thy grace.

But when thou dost anneal in glass thy story,
Making thy life to shine within
The holy Preacher's, then the life and glory
More rev'rend grows, and more doth win:
Which else shows wat'rish, bleak and thin.

Doctrine and life, colours and light, in one
When they combine and mingle, bring
A strong regard and awe: but speech alone
Doth vanish like a flaring thing,
And in the ear, not conscience ring.

George Herbert's inscription above his front door.

TRINITY SUNDAY

Lord, who hast form'd me out of Mud
And hast redeemed me through the Blood,
And sanctified me to do good;

Purge all my Sins done heretofore:
For I confess my heavy score:
And I will strive to sin no more.

Enrich my Heart, Mouth, Hands in me,
With Faith, with Hope, with Charity;
That I may run, rise, rest with Thee.

VIRTUE

Sweet Day, so cool, so calm, so bright,
The Bridal of the Earth and Sky,
The Dew shall weep thy fall tonight;
For thou must die.

Sweet Rose, whose hue angry and brave
Bids the rash Gazer wipe his Eye,
Thy Root is ever in its grave,
And thou must die.

Sweet Spring, full of sweet Days and Roses,
A Box where Sweets compacted lie,
My Musick shews ye have your closes,
And all must die.

Only a sweet and virtuous Soul,
Like season'd Timber, never gives;
But though the whole World turn to coal,
Then chiefly lives.

THE ELIXIR

Teach me, my God and King
In all things thee to see,
And what I do in any thing,
To do it as for thee;

Not rudely as a Beast
To run into an action,
But still to make thee prepossest,
And give it his Perfection.

A Man that looks on Glass,
On it may stay his Eye;
Or if he pleases, through it pass,
And then the Heav'n spy.

All may of thee partake:
Nothing can be so mean,
With which his Tincture (for thy sake)
Will not grow bright and clean.

A Servant with this Clause
Makes Drudgery divine:
Who sweeps a Room, as for thy Laws,
Makes that and th'Action fine.

This is the famous Stone,
That turneth all to Gold:
For that which God doth touch and own,
Cannot for less be told.

JESU

Jesu is in my Heart, his sacred Name
Is deeply carved there; but th'other week
A great Affliction broke the little frame,
Ev'n all to pieces; which I went to seek:
And first I found the corner, where was J,
After, where ES, and next where U was graved.
When I had got these Parcels, instantly
I sat me down to spell them, and perceived
That to my broken Heart he was I ease you,
And to my whole is JESU.

THE FLOWER [first two and last two stanzas]

How fresh, O Lord, how sweet and clean
Are thy returns! ev'n as the flowers in spring;
To which, besides their own demean,
The late-past frosts tributes of pleasure bring.
    Grief melts away
    Like snow in May
As if there were no such cold thing.

Who would have thought my shrivelled heart
Could have recovered greenness? It was gone
Quite underground; as flowers depart
To see their mother-root, when they have blown;
    Where they together
    All the hard weather,
Dead to the world, keep house unknown.

And now in age I bud again,
After so many deaths I live and write;
I once more smell the dew and rain,
And relish versing: O my only light,
    It cannot be
    That I am he
On whom thy tempests fell all night.

These are thy wonders, Lord of love,
To make us see we are but flowers that glide:
Which when we once can find and prove,
Thou hast a garden for us, where to bide.
    Who would be more,
    Swelling through store,
Forfeit their Paradise by their pride.

George Herbert's church at Bemerton.

Barbara Murray

ENNUI

The landscape viewed,
The stubble sod,
The book read,
The road trod.

The scraped plate,
The cut knot,
The shut gate—
The wife forgot.

AT HIS GOING: JANUARY 28, 1984

One muffled word; without a look you went then,
Firmly closed the door.
Well, you had planned, were waiting for it even,
Of that I was sure.
You could not call the courage to propose it
In a calmer, kinder way.
Perhaps you thought it certain I'd oppose it,
Urge you to stay.

Time was, in all those other, earlier goings,
In my great distress
I'd plead, for children left without a father,
For myself, husbandless.
You heeded, did your duty, yet you could not
Your stock of love increase.
Now my last word of love I speak (though I would not):
Go: be at peace.

SHE REMEMBERS EARLY LOVE

We met at the station;
There at my sight
A sweet smile he gave me,
A smile of delight.

One look like this only
In memory I have;
I take that look with me
Down to the grave.

    1984

IN PRAISE OF WOMEN

Women are steadfast, women kind,
Women act with heart and mind,
And if I had another life.
I'd be a man, and take a wife.

    1984

LETTER ON 'A FEW GREEN LEAVES'

Dear Marian,
        No more Barbara Pym!
I've found the going awfully grim!
Such people! All so unappealing,
their desultory talk concealing
a poverty of heart and mind
that in true life I never find.
Creeping along from day to day
fearful of what the neighbours say,
of new experience terrified—
(See Chapter 18, The Bus Ride—
"humiliated," "embarrassed," "confused"—
this is the language that is used.
Why? Emma didn't KNOW THE FARE.)
Such timid souls make me despair.
No wrongs, no rights, no ties that bind,
sins of omission the only kind.
Alas! I simply do not care
what Emma eats, or when, or where,
who brings what to the Jumble Sale
or gets a letter in the mail.
I could go on and on—enough!
I'll sum it up in language rough—
No STYLE, no CHARACTER, no PLOT!
A few dried twigs was all I got.

    1984

WORDS

Words of beauty, you slide upon me like silk upon skin;
With you I begin.
Intricate words, I tangle you and unlace you.
Words of truth, embrace you.
Gentle words, like pebbles I smooth and turn you,
Passionate words, burn you!

Joyful words, I sing to you,
Trills and adornment I bring to you.
Sorrowful words, I suffer and weep and mourn you,
Proud words, scorn you!
But kind words, you my treasures till night I keep,
Then wrapping me with you as with a blanket, I sleep.

    September 1985

AT NIGHT ON THE GREEN

One floodlight high in an oak tree—commonplace thing!—
Transfigures the leaves of one bough into gold more gorgeous
Than oak-garlands hammered fine for the Macedonian king.

?1985

THE RITUAL

I am out at the usual time, walking my dog.
He is there at the end of the road, pacing again,
a thin, frail, upright, solitary man.
Thirty feet up the street and thirty down,
Then back as he sees me coming, into his drive,
where he turns to the road and stands as I walk past.
I smile; he smiles shyly. "Good evening." "Good evening," we say.
Could those be the only words he has spoken all day?
Is he still there, pacing, those nights when I walk a different way?

September 1985

MAPLES

Did you ever think to see such resplendent dress
as the full golden skirts of the maples against the sky?
Stay then to gaze while you may on that sumptuousness,
for when next you go by
every leaf will be taken,
each glowing robe shaken
in tatters of gold to lie.

    October 1985

DESPITERS

Weed in the asphalt,
plant in cracked pavement,
stem under stone.
Twisted, still striving
or stunted, half thriving
yet showing brave bloom there—
we called them 'Despiters'.

I too unthrifty,
fixing my roots in
poor soil and little
between wall and stone—
pushing pale leaves up,
budding and blossoming;
I the Despiter.

    May 1986

SUMMER RAIN

Having just returned from a hot dry country,
I went out to clip the hedges—the morning was soft,
and after a little while came the sweet rain falling
in drops at first, then a steady gentle downpour
that soaked my shirt through, showered my cheeks and lips
when I turned up my face to the sky.

I stood there grateful, still clipping and blessing the rain.
And I thought of you too, my mother, who taught me to love it—
(a gardener you were, and to such rain is kindly and welcome).
For it came back to me most clearly how when we were children
with your blessing we put on our swimsuits and ran outside
to dance with joy in the warm, soft summer rain.

    August 1989

TREASURES

Eye to the chink, he peered through intently.
Gilded in death lay the chamber of kings.
Glintings of treasures sucked out his breath then—
'What do you see there?' 'Wonderful things!'

No less astounded I stand in the woodland,
fastening my eyes on the splendours around
where gold, copper, apricot, scarlet, magenta
gleam from the branches, lie dazzling the ground.

Unendurable beauty that cannot be plundered,
you fade in the hand, are not crafted nor sold.
Yet safe in the mind's eye I'll mount this exhibit,
and there view my treasure, my glory, my gold.

    10/91

TO ALBERT AT CHRISTMAS

It is no angel choir you lead
But shepherds, humble folk indeed.
With patient care you coax us on
Till all our hesitation's gone,
And in our souls at least we find
The perfect strains you have in mind.
Oh, if upon our Piney hill
Our music could but match your skill,
We'd sing, as angels did for them,
Shepherds of hilly Bethlehem.

    1993

UNDER THE SWEETGUM TREE

in summer how hard to accept
that these multitudinous shapes suspended above me
will one day turn to the color of dying, and then
each leaf, loosing its hold at some silent signal,
will fall. None will be left, not one.

How frame the mind to foresee that, in summer?

In winter I strain to envision
that from under the bleak brown bones of this skeleton tree
will push out shining buds that prick at the sky.
They parting in turn upon numberless points of green
will unfold their tenderness, spread like luminous wings.

It is asking too much to believe this, in winter.

    July 1994

HAIKU

Full moon after rain
Lights droplets on a pine bough
Into tiny moons.

   8.21.94

A friend is taken,
They laid her in the garden.
Rest well, rest well now.

   8.21.94

HAIKU: FURMAN

In milk-blue water
Three maples burning, burning,
Though so deeply drowned.

O YELLOW-SHAFTED FLICKER

O yellow-shafted flicker!
There you lie broken at the side of the road.
Your beak gapes stilly; your eyes are dull.
And one torn wing's flung open like a fan,
strong golden shafts against the black and white,
a cruel celebration of your naming;
a last array of beauty.

O yellow-shafted flicker!

    August 1996

NATURE NOTE, THANKSGIVING 1994

The heron is back, bird of my paradise,
the great blue heron I love beyond all birds.
Softly I came upon him by the verge,
and he the wary lifted himself at once,
and with deliberate strokes of those great wings
that curve and beat with such slow sinuous strength,
flew off across the center of the lake
a foot above the water. O delight!
The low fall sun struck gold on his pale face,
gilding his bill, making his plumage glow
a soft aethereal blue. I gazed after him
till he was gone, and went away still wondering.

Barbara Murray
juvenilia

ICARE
by Philippe Desportes

Icare est chut ici, le jeune audacieux,
Qui pour voler au ciel eut assez de courage:
Ici tomba son corps dégarni de plumage,
Laissant tous braves coeurs de sa chute envieux.

Ô bienheureux travail d'un esprit glorieux,
Qui tire un si grand gain d'un si petit dommage.
Ô bienheureux malheur plein de tant d'avantage,
Qu'il rende le vaincu des ans victorieux!

Un chemin si nouveau n'étonna sa jeunesse,
Le pouvoir lui faillit, mais non la hardiesse,
Il eut pour le bruler des astres le plus beau;

Il mourut poursuivant une haute aventure;
Le ciel fut son désir, la mer sa sépulture;
Est-il plus beau dessein, ou plus riche tombeau?

ICARUS
Translation by Barbara Murray, June 1950

Icarus lies here, hushed, who daring all
Strove in courageous flight for lofty things.
Here fell his body, stripped of feathered wings,
Leaving all brave hearts envious of his fall.

Joyful attempt of one who knew no fears,
Whose flight was so small loss, and so great gain
In glory, such as made it not in vain,
And gave the vanquished his victorious years.

Of this new way, his youth was undismayed,
Strength failed him, yet his courage could not fade.
What mattered heat, when stars were lovelier?

From soaring flight he came at last to doom,
The sky his high desire, the sea his tomb.
Could there be nobler aim, or richer sepulchre?

[on reverse of "Icare"]

CANTERBURY PLAINS, April 1950

And now we turn on to a rougher road . . .
This is the country; and how beautiful
The quiet fields, and white road stretching on
To the faint-hazed and purple-hollowed hills.
Lulléd the cows lie in the sleepy grass,
And autumn poplars stand up yellow-splashed
Along the unkempt hedges. And how deep
Calm drowsiness and peace lie over all!

Time as a rule is hardly noticed here,
Does not intrude himself as in the town,
With hard and jangly strokes that clamour out
Above the noise of motor'd things, and people,
Cutting the day, dividing it in pieces,
But is content that Nature be the clock
Which marks the silent passing of the seasons.
Ringing the changes in the shooting leaf,
The green maturity; the slow rich ripening
Of cereals to mellow gold, and then
The stark, gaunt, sparkling, handsome days that follow
When frost spikes leaves and silvers the black branches
[end of page]

[on reverse of "Icarus"]

THE GULL (after G. M. Hopkins)

High in the sun-soft sky fleet-flying, O lovely one
Swift-swept wings clear-curving in the shaft-shimmer sun
Proud-plumed and graceful, O most graceful, Sea-kings' daughter
Who tiring, even you tiring, drooping when day is done,
Float lightly, feather-fluffed, on the silk-sheer shifting water.

    April 1950

YOU WHO ARE GAY

You who are gay and ever laughing-hearted,
Know well now what you do to challenge Death.
From those who seek Him he is soon departed,
And, fickle, stops the unsuspecting breath.

But is it spite, and are those snatched from gladness
To lie in thick-wrapped darkness evermore?
Or does Death take them ere they thought of sadness,
To show them joy they have not known before?

    May 1950

www.ingramcontent.com/pod-product-compliance
Lightning Source LLC
Chambersburg PA
CBHW070750050426
42449CB00010B/2411